Prayers

for

Hope &

Healing

Prayers & Promises
for
Hope &
Healing

BARBOUR
PUBLISHING

© 2012 by Barbour Publishing, Inc.

Print ISBN 978-1-62029-171-9

eBook Editions:
Adobe Digital Edition (.epub) 978-1-62029-546-5
Kindle and MobiPocket Edition (.prc) 978-1-62029-545-8

Readings are taken from *Prayers and Promises*, *Prayers and Promises in Times of Loss*, *Prayers and Promises for Women*, and *Prayers and Promises for Mothers*, published by Barbour Publishing, Inc.

Scripture quotations marked KJV are taken from the King James Version of the Bible.

Scripture quotations marked NIV are taken from the HOLY BIBLE, NEW INTERNATIONAL VERSION®. NIV®. Copyright © 1973, 1978, 1984, 2011 by Biblica, Inc.™ Used by permission. All rights reserved worldwide.

Scripture quotations marked NKJV are taken from the New King James Version®. Copyright © 1982 by Thomas Nelson, Inc. Used by permission. All rights reserved.

Scripture quotations marked AMP are taken from the Amplified® Bible, © 1954, 1958, 1962, 1964, 1965, 1987 by The Lockman Foundation. Used by permission.

Scripture quotations marked NLT are taken from the *Holy Bible*. New Living Translation copyright© 1996, 2004, 2007 by Tyndale House Foundation. Used by permission of Tyndale House Publishers, Inc. Carol Stream, Illinois 60188. All rights reserved.

Scripture quotations marked NASB are taken from the New American Standard Bible, © 1960, 1962, 1963, 1968, 1971, 1972, 1973, 1975, 1977, 1995 by The Lockman Foundation. Used by permission.

Published by Barbour Publishing, Inc., P.O. Box 719, Uhrichsville, Ohio 44683, www.barbourbooks.com

Our mission is to publish and distribute inspirational products offering exceptional value and biblical encouragement to the masses.

 Member of the
Evangelical Christian
Publishers Association

Printed in the United States of America.

Contents

God brings each Christian many blessings, but none of us can avoid pain in our lives. Since the Fall, humanity has struggled to understand why physical and emotional havoc occur.

Many thoughts fill us when we're hurting. As our minds race along painful paths, communication with God can become a sacrifice instead of a joy. When we most need God, we are often furthest from Him. But because prayerlessness harms us on our spiritual walk, we need to make efforts to speak with the Creator.

Those who hurt sometimes need a starting place for their own prayers. In these pages are petitions, words of encouragement, and praises that can act as a basis for personal prayer or stand alone. However you use them, we hope they will draw you to God. He is always close at hand, willing to lift up the hurting heart and bring healing to those who believe in His promises.

Whether you are struggling with guilt or fear or loss today, grab hold of a truth in scripture and share a heartfelt prayer.

Rejoice always, pray without ceasing.
1 THESSALONIANS 5:16–17 NKJV

Care

A Father's Love

For whom the LORD loveth he correcteth;
even as a father the son in whom he delighteth.
PROVERBS 3:12 KJV

*O*nly a parent bothers to lovingly tell a child that he or she has done wrong. Most people don't know the youngster well enough or care deeply enough to take the risk that comes with correction.

Thank You, Father God, for caring enough about me to tell me when I'm headed in the wrong direction. Even when I've gotten into a real mess and ignored Your warnings, You still pull me up, take me back to the place where I went wrong, and start me on a new path.

I appreciate Your love, even when the correction is painful. Thank You for being a loving Father to me.

*Yes, happy (blessed, fortunate, prosperous, to be envied)
are the people whose God is the Lord!*

PSALM 144:15 AMP

*J*ust knowing You, Lord, is my greatest blessing. Whether life is calm and peaceful or filled with trials, when I rest in You, I am in the right place. Joy, security, and love come from Your hand, and nothing I could buy fills the empty places of my heart as Your Spirit does.

Thank You, Lord, for every blessing You have granted me. Since You care about all of my life, down to the loss of each hair on my head, I live securely. Nothing that happens to me today—or any day—lies beyond Your plan and power. I want to remember that every second of this day.

In God

*For the LORD will be at your side
and will keep your foot from being snared.*

PROVERBS 3:26 NIV

*N*o matter what my situation, Lord, You promise I don't have to worry about facing sudden disaster. While those who pay You no mind fear the future, anyone whose confidence lies in You remains safe.

I know that doesn't mean I won't face trials, but You promise to go through them with me. Since You know the beginning and end of my life, I can have confidence that You will care for all my in-between needs. Thank You, Lord, for keeping me from being snared. Because I believe in You, Your plans bring me through life triumphantly.

Keep my trust always in You, Jesus. That's where it *should* be. After all, You are my confidence.

GOD'S WATCHFUL CARE

The LORD watches over the foreigner
and sustains the fatherless and the widow,
but he frustrates the ways of the wicked.

PSALM 146:9 NIV

Lord, I'm so glad You watch over the weak, the downhearted, and the ones left out by the world. When life feels unfair, it's comforting to know You have not left me. If a wicked person seeks to harm me, You will intervene.

Right now, I feel so powerless, Lord. Help me trust in You for direction for my future. This verse isn't just a line in the Bible—it's a promise of Your care for me. Thank You for caring when I am in trouble. I need Your help right now, Jesus. I'm glad You're watching over me today.

No Concern

*Y*ou know me so well, Lord. How many of my worries focus on tomorrow! Fears of things that may not even happen and concerns about others that eventually turn out right can paralyze my life.

Your words remind me I can only live in today. Tomorrow must care for itself, because looking ahead in fear wastes my days. Yet I need never worry because You control my life. No twenty-four hours, present or future, contain anything that surprises You. Nothing lies outside Your power.

When I face agitated thoughts and doubts, I need only persistently ask You to care for whatever lies ahead. Then I need no longer concern myself. Help me turn to You alone, O Lord.

Make a Call

As for me, I call to God, and the LORD saves me.
Evening, morning and noon I cry out in distress,
and he hears my voice.

PSALM 55:16–17 NIV

When I feel distressed, I don't have to listen to my own voice and fear that no one cares. Your ear is cocked toward my every cry, Lord. No matter what the hour, You listen to all I ask.

You not only lend an ear, you answer my cries and save me from every problem. I've seen it in the past, when problems have been solved more simply than I imagined or never really materialized at all. When I look to You in my distress, You work in amazing ways.

Thank You for Your loving response, Lord. I'm glad I made a call to You.

And I will pray the Father,
and he shall give you another Comforter,
that he may abide with you for ever. . . .
I will not leave you comfortless:
I will come to you.

JOHN 14:16, 18 KJV

*L*ord, You know that sometimes I reject Your promises. When I am really lonely and depressed, nothing seems to make me feel better. I know You are with me; I know You care when no one else cares—but some days even that is not enough. The fault is in me, not in You. On days like that, remind me that although Your promises are free for the taking, I still need to accept them, to claim them, and then to live in faith that they are mine. No gift is truly ours until we open it and accept it in thankfulness and joy.

ONE HAIR

But the very hairs of your head are all numbered.
MATTHEW 10:30 KJV

I know this verse is an illustration of how important I am to You, Father. If You care about such a small thing as one hair, I can only imagine Your concern when I am sick or suffering a loss. Bad things will come my way in life, but I am secure in Your love that never fails. I am constantly blessed by Your care and concern. I am so important to You that even the hairs of my head are all numbered.

Comfort

MOUNT ZION

They that trust in the LORD
shall be as mount Zion,
which cannot be removed,
but abideth for ever.
As the mountains are round about Jerusalem,
so the LORD is round about his people
from henceforth even for ever.

PSALM 125:1–2 KJV

I come to You seeking a safe haven, Father, a town nestled in a mountain chain, safe from any attack from the outside world. I come seeking peace and the freedom to follow Your way. Of course I know there is no such place, geographically speaking; Jerusalem fell often, mountains or not.

What I seek is Your presence, Father. I trust in You, and You have promised to be with me forever, surrounding me with Your sheltering arms. I seek to be Your mountain—faithful forever, secure in Your love, unmovable in times of peril.

[God] comforts us in all our troubles,
so that we can comfort those in any trouble
with the comfort we ourselves
receive from God.

2 CORINTHIANS 1:4 NIV

I'm glad, Lord, that Your comfort has a purpose. I've learned so much about You in my suffering, and I'd like to pass it on.

All the people who have been there for me, encouraging me when I felt low, have blessed me deeply. I want to give that to others. Help me share Your strength and comfort with anyone who hurts today. You don't give me anything—not even hard times—to hoard.

You've also offered me consolation straight from Your heart, Lord. Even when no one else could help, I felt Your love healing my tenderest spots. Thank You, Jesus, for all Your love. Without it, how would I have made it through?

I will not leave you comfortless:
I will come to you.

John 14:18 kjv

A world without You, Lord, would be comfortless indeed. Now that You've entered my heart and filled me with Your love, I can hardly imagine not having the hope of Your love to guide me.

When I face trials that seem to separate me from You, I still trust that if I draw close to You, You will be my comfort. When life seems darkest, You will come to me, bringing Your peace.

No one can comfort like You, Lord. Reach into my soul today. I need Your Spirit's consolation.

THE DEPTHS OF GRIEF

For I am persuaded, that neither death,
nor life, nor angels, nor principalities,
nor powers, nor things present,
nor things to come, nor height,
nor depth, nor any other creature,
shall be able to separate us from
the love of God,
which is in Christ Jesus our Lord.

ROMANS 8:38–39 KJV

I am alone, Father, in the midst of a crowd of friends and relatives who have come to comfort me. I will not be consoled. I will not smile at the grandchildren; I will not joy in the sunshine. I feel only partially here because the one I love is dead.

I am loved. I know that. No matter how I feel or act, my friends and family love me. You love me. But for now, I will not be comforted. Perhaps tomorrow. I know You understand.

COMFORT

Blessed be. . .the God of all comfort;
who comforteth us in all our tribulation,
that we may be able to comfort them
which are in any trouble,
by the comfort wherewith
we ourselves are comforted of God.

2 CORINTHIANS 1:3–4 KJV

*W*hat a blessing it is, Lord, to experience comfort that comes directly from Your
heart. No matter what my troubles, Your
peace reaches the hurting places within me.

Help me to pass comfort on to those
who are also in need. Open my heart to Your
wisdom and gentleness, and let the light of
compassion burn brightly in my life because
of the solace I have received.

NEVER-FAILING MERCY

But if the wicked will turn from
all his sins that he hath committed,
and keep all my statutes,
and do that which is lawful and right,
he shall surely live,
he shall not die.

EZEKIEL 18:21 KJV

*F*ather, I know that on my own I am incapable of keeping Your law perfectly, but Your mercy never ends, and Your justice never fails. You know my soul intimately and welcome me with joy every time I repent and turn back to You.

Have mercy upon me, merciful Father. Pour Your Spirit down on me, bringing me comfort on the worst of my days. Remind me that You will never let me go far from Your side, for You desire my presence even more than I desire Yours. You will go to any length to save me.

*"Blessed are those who mourn,
for they shall be comforted."*

MATTHEW 5:4 NKJV

I don't really think of mourning as a blessing, Jesus. I'd rather avoid it than embrace it. Yet if I never experienced sorrow, I'd also never feel the comfort that surpasses all this earth can offer. Your love reaches places inside me no human affection can touch. When I've deeply hurt, Your Spirit has consoled me in powerful, unexpected ways.

It's unlikely that I'll ever want to mourn, but when it happens, I know You stand right with me in the pain. Thank You for healing my heart and giving me relief I can share with others. You alone give perfect peace to the human heart. Thank You, Jesus.

Break forth into joy, sing together,
ye waste places of Jerusalem:
for the LORD hath comforted his people,
he hath redeemed Jerusalem.

ISAIAH 52:9 KJV

*E*ven when nothing else brings me comfort, Your salvation consoles me, Jesus. It's not hard for me to imagine where I'd be without Your love—and it would be nowhere good. I wandered in a wasteland before Your love touched me.

Though I struggle now, I know all will eventually work for good. What seems so terrible today will not last forever. Already, piece by piece, positive things are returning to my life. I will never forget my loss, but You bring me new experiences to comfort and cheer or an old truth to remind me of Your love.

Soon I will know Your comfort more completely and will break into a joyous song. My heart's already tuning up for it.

Contentment

WORLDLY CARES

Therefore take no thought,
saying, What shall we eat?
or, What shall we drink? or,
Wherewithal shall we be clothed? . . .
for your heavenly Father knoweth
that ye have need of all these things.

MATTHEW 6:31–32 KJV

You sent Your disciples out into the world with nothing but Your teaching, Lord, confident that their physical needs would be met if they sought the kingdom of God and God's righteousness, depending on the Father for everything else. To Your glory. . .that's exactly how they lived the remainder of their lives.

I wish my faith were that strong. I wish I could leave my concerns behind and dedicate my life to Your work. Forgive me my worldly attachments and anxieties. Help me seek Your kingdom so I may live as a good example of Your never-failing care and concern.

Waiting for
the Reward

Let not thine heart envy sinners:
but be thou in the fear of the LORD
all the day long.
For surely there is an end;
and thine expectation shall not be cut off.

PROVERBS 23:17–18 KJV

Sometimes I wonder, Lord: Why do sinners seem to flourish while Your people struggle to support their families? Is it better for me to be poor? Surely there are those better off than I who are righteous; couldn't I be one of them? I get tired and discouraged.

But You promise that all bad things come to an end; my heart's desire will one day be mine. Until then, give me contentment with the blessings I have and faith in tomorrow.

A Broken Spirit

A broken spirit drieth the bones.
PROVERBS 17:22 KJV

If a broken spirit dries the bones, Lord, about now mine should be dust. I'm not at all content with my situation, and my heart is down in the dumps. Turn my spirit toward You again, where I can find the joy and contentment I'm missing. May I feel Your Spirit touch my heart, so that I may bring good to those I see each day. Help me rejoice in You, no matter what is going on in my life. I don't want sin to turn me into a pile of dry bones, and I don't want to share that attitude with others.

Pour Your blessed balm on my aching heart, O Lord.

CONTENTED!

The fear of the LORD leads to life,
and he who has it will abide in satisfaction;
he will not be visited with evil.

PROVERBS 19:23 NKJV

This isn't a popular idea, Lord: few people like the idea of fearing You. But You are powerful beyond anything our hearts and minds can imagine, and wise people—those who believe in You—know You deserve respect and obedience.

I need not go in fear of You, though. You have made me Your child, and that makes all the difference. You've offered me rest in You, and I've accepted. How awesome that You no longer want my fear but my faith. In You, my heart need never dread. I'm trusting in my Lord and rest content.

A MERRY HEART

A merry heart doeth good like a medicine.
PROVERBS 17:22 KJV

I know a woman who overflows with a merry heart, Lord. She smiles continuously and laughs loudly, infecting everyone around her with the giggles. She makes everyone feel good about themselves, no matter what the situation, because her concern for others is genuine. She is a very sick woman but enjoys every moment of life, whether it is full of joy or pain, and shrugs off her illnesses. I frankly do not know how she does it, but I do believe her happy heart has lengthened her life. Lord, I wish I could live in continuous joy the way she does. I would like to be remembered for my laugh but am afraid not enough people have heard it. I would love to be content no matter what comes my way. Keep this woman healthy as well as happy. The world needs her.

All the days of the afflicted are evil:
but he that is of a merry heart
hath a continual feast.

PROVERBS 15:15 KJV

I have been afflicted in my lifetime, as have most women, but You helped me walk out of affliction and invited me to Your continual feast. Right now I am still at Your banquet, but I know affliction will come again. Right now I am content and comfortable, enjoying life to its fullest. I don't know if I will feel that way when trials come to me again, because I don't really have a merry heart. Like most people, I am happiest when things are going nicely, but when things go wrong, my heart is not so merry. Help me get over this nagging self-doubt, Father. Remind me that Your blessings are forever and I have nothing to fear. Give me a merry heart, I pray.

"Fret Not"

Fret not thyself because of evildoers,
neither be thou envious against
the workers of iniquity.
For they shall soon be cut down
like the grass,
and wither as the green herb.

PSALM 37:1–2 KJV

hank You for Your promise, Lord, that tells me that even the most wicked people cannot take the world out of Your hands. Before cold spiritual weather withers their hearts, may I reach out to evildoers with Your good news. Let none be cut down or wither because I would not share the contentment I find in You.

Not that I speak in respect of want:
for I have learned, in whatsoever state I am,
therewith to be content.

Philippians 4:11 KJV

Father, some days I want so many things—I feel like a little child, stomping my foot and demanding my way. At the time, all those desires seem so necessary; yet when I stop to think, I know they don't truly matter. They are material and temporal and of no value in heaven.

Fill me with so much contentment that my family will be blessed with understanding this principle. Teach us to be satisfied with Your provision for our needs. Help me realize that my wants are temporary and of little importance. Let me lean against You, Lord, relaxed in the knowledge that You will care for me.

Encouragement

PRISONS WITHOUT BARS

Bring my soul out of prison,
that I may praise thy name:
the righteous shall compass me about;
for thou shalt deal bountifully with me.

PSALM 142:7 KJV

*F*ather, we are all prisoners of something. I may not be behind bars, but neither am I totally free. Whether I am a prisoner of sin, a prisoner of fear, a prisoner of poverty, or a prisoner of poor health, I ask You to hear my prayer and give me Your perfect freedom.

Let my brothers and sisters give me guidance and support as I struggle with my personal prison, showing me the way to freedom through their love and compassion. Then, when I am free, let me give the same help to others who need my encouragement in their struggles.

FIGHTING DISCOURAGEMENT

*"Then you will have success if
you are careful to observe the decrees and laws
that the LORD gave Moses for Israel.
Be strong and courageous.
Do not be afraid or discouraged."*

1 CHRONICLES 22:13 NIV

*D*iscouragement comes easily to me, Lord, when I feel sad. Sorrow makes me feel so empty inside. It's as if I've lost my way for a while.

But You remind me that my obedience to Your laws, because I love You, will give me strength in You. I have no reason to dread. Just as You were faithful to Moses and Israel, You will keep me, too.

When I feel weak, Your power can fill me, Jesus. Neither fear nor discouragement needs to control my heart. You'll win the fight against fear and depression, if I only trust in You.

Encouraged!

*Be of good courage,
and He shall strengthen your heart,
all you who hope in the LORD.*

PSALM 31:24 NKJV

*W*here can I find strength to go on in trials? Only in You, Lord. When my heart falters and I cannot imagine where to turn, I lift my face to You and suddenly receive the energy to go on. Your Spirit leads me in the right direction, even when every map and compass seem to fail.

Other paths only seem to offer hope. For a while I might feel encouraged, but no other faith, no human or physical solution, has Your eternal strength. Everything humanity comes up with falls short of Your heart-empowering ability, Lord.

Thank You, Jesus, for lifting me up. I need Your courage filling my life if I'm to live for You.

FAITHFUL

A friend loveth at all times,
and a brother is born for adversity.

PROVERBS 17:17 KJV

Thank You, Lord God, for the faithful friends who have stood by me in adversity. Sometimes they seem more like brothers or sisters than my own siblings do. When that happens, my friends and I know it's because Your love fills our hearts. Thank You for giving me such relationships.

I, too, want to be a friend at all times, the way my friends have been to me. Help me choose my friends wisely and stand by them when they need encouragement or help. When life challenges their faith, I want to be standing right at their sides.

CLOSER THAN
A BROTHER

A man that hath friends
must shew himself friendly:
and there is a friend that
sticketh closer than a brother.

PROVERBS 18:24 KJV

Thank You, Jesus, for bringing me this friend. We've shared so much through Your love. Now help me follow Your example and stick closer than a brother to my friend in need.

Though Your touch may seem distant, help my friend cling to Your love. I trust that You will stick near us both as we walk together through this dark time.

Strengthen me to stay close to her during these struggles and show her Your love. By Your power, guide me to reach out. Use me to help meet my friend's needs.

Bless my friend, O Lord.

VICTORY

Therefore, my beloved brethren,
be ye stedfast, unmoveable,
always abounding in the work of the Lord,
forasmuch as ye know that your labour
is not in vain in the Lord.

1 CORINTHIANS 15:58 KJV

In my daily work I rarely experience victory. I clean up one mess and move on to the next, knowing even greater messes are just around the corner. I never really seem to get anywhere, to win any battles, or to see anything truly completed. There are precious few victories in my work. But You encourage me to hang in there and keep on working for You, because You have already won the victory in the most important battle of all—the battle for my soul. My daily problems come and go; yet if I remain steadfast and dedicated, doing the work You have given me to do, I am confident that my reward awaits me. Thank You, Lord.

I the LORD thy God will hold thy right hand,
saying unto thee,
Fear not; I will help thee.

ISAIAH 41:13 KJV

I watched two children today, Lord—one afraid, the other reaching out a hand to help the fearful one. Tears came to my eyes as I thought of all the times that You've been there for me when I was afraid. You've held my hand and helped me in some difficult situations. With Your help I've walked when I might have fallen.

Not once have You ever laughed at me or told me how silly I was to be fearful. Help me to be this understanding to others—to encourage rather than discourage. I want to take their hands and walk with them, as You've taken mine to walk with me.

Being an Encourager

Now we exhort you, brethren,
warn them that are unruly,
comfort the feebleminded, support the weak,
be patient toward all men.

1 Thessalonians 5:14 KJV

Whether I like it or not, I am an example to others, Lord. How many times have I failed to do what this verse commands? I'm not always patient. I don't take time to comfort or support those who need it most.

Day by day, moment by moment, I want to improve. I want to instruct my family on the need to be there for others, to encourage in whatever way is needed. Your Word says I have to do this by example.

The little ways count, Lord. Help me learn that to grow as an encourager I can start with the small things as I comfort others and build from there.

Forgiveness

SHARED LOVE

*"For God did not send his Son
into the world to condemn the world,
but to save the world through him."*

JOHN 3:17 NIV

I've needed Your salvation, not judgment, in this time of trial, Lord. How thankful I am that You have not condemned my failings, but when I've hurt, You have drawn near.

When life has been tense, it's sometimes been easier for me to want to judge and condemn instead of lifting up another hurting heart. Thank You for encouraging me, instead, to pass on the love You've shown me. You have not given me the role of judge or savior, but I can pass on the message of forgiveness that You gave. Help me reach out to empty hearts today and share the love that's meant so much to me.

Repentance

If we confess our sins,
he is faithful and just
to forgive us our sins,
and to cleanse us from
all unrighteousness.

1 John 1:9 KJV

From the days when I first came to know You, O God, I believed Your promise that forgiveness required only simple, honest confession and repentance.

But how my soul struggles to daily frame those words of repentance. Willfulness and rebellion make my confessions stick in my throat. Though I ache to admit my faults, sin holds me back.

Free me, Savior, to open my soul to You. May my heart show me my error and prompt me to quickly seek pardon. Cleanse me from all sin, and glorify Yourself in my life.

Anger and God's Forgiveness

Let all bitterness, and wrath,
and anger, and clamour,
and evil speaking, be put away from you,
with all malice: And be ye kind one to another,
tenderhearted, forgiving one another,
even as God for Christ's sake hath forgiven you.

Ephesians 4:31–32 KJV

*F*ather, You have taken my sins and put them far away from me, as if I had never sinned, for the sake of Jesus, my Redeemer. Yet still I fall victim to anger, wrath, and malice toward others, despite Your loving example. I live in a world full of anger, and I find forgiving difficult. In times of violent emotions, help me remember Your unending forgiveness and treat others with the kindness and compassion that You show to me every day of my life.

God's Forgiveness

For the LORD your God is
gracious and merciful,
and will not turn away
his face from you,
if ye return unto him.

2 CHRONICLES 30:9 KJV

*H*ow far I have strayed from You, Lord. It hurts to know how I've harmed You and those I love.

You've promised that if I return to You, You will not turn away. Forgive my sin, Lord, and help me make things right with those I've hurt. Help them to forgive my wrongs, too.

Turn my heart from evil, Jesus, and help me be more like You each day. Put this sin in my past—forever.

As far as the east is from the west,
so far hath he removed our
transgressions from us.

PSALM 103:12 KJV

I can't seem to let go of some guilt, Lord. Thank You for reminding me that when You remove a wrong from my life, it's gone for good.

Help me to trust in Your words and put them to work in my life. When Satan reminds me of my past, let me drop the memory of that sin into the ocean of Your love.

Jesus, thank You for showing Your love for me by being the way to forgiveness. Without You there would be no distance at all between me and my sin.

*"The LORD is slow to anger,
abounding in love and
forgiving sin and rebellion.
Yet he does not leave the guilty unpunished;
he punishes the children for the sin of
the parents to the third and fourth generation."*

NUMBERS 14:18 NIV

Hurt that overwhelms makes it easy for us to be angry in everything, Lord. We have less patience with others, situations become stressful, and it's hard to keep life under control.

Thank You for reminding me of Your own nature, which forgave me for so much. Since You want me to become just like You, You call me not to accept quick anger but to avoid all wrongdoing that deserves punishment.

I know I can't do this on my own, so forgive me and fill me with Your Spirit, Lord. I need patience and love in this time of trouble.

MERCIFUL FORGIVENESS

Who is a God like you,
who pardons sin and forgives
the transgression of the remnant
of his inheritance?
You do not stay angry forever
but delight to show mercy.

MICAH 7:18 NIV

*P*eople in pain can generate a lot of anger, Lord. Disappointment, doubt, and fear cause us to strike out at others, even though we know this is not right.

If anger stirs my emotions, remind me of Your forgiveness and mercy, poured out into my heart. Help me grab hold of them and pass them on to others.

I don't want to start a fight and produce bad feelings that last forever, Lord—or even for a while. Instead, I want to forgive and share Your mercy, even when there is still so much pain.

JESUS' EXAMPLE

*If we confess our sins,
he is faithful and just and
will forgive us our sins and purify us
from all unrighteousness.*

1 JOHN 1:9 NIV

When I look at forgiveness, I look at You, Jesus. Even before I had any idea You existed, You willingly died for me. Though I couldn't have done anything to make you pardon me, Your love prompted You to offer me Your grace.

Help me reflect Your love, Lord, by forgiving those who wrong me. In my own power, I weakly want revenge. But through Your Spirit, poured out in my life, I follow Your loving example.

Forgive me for all my sins, Lord, and make me faithful and pure in You.

God's Faithfulness

INFINITE STRENGTH

I will call upon the LORD,
who is worthy to be praised:
so shall I be saved from mine enemies.

PSALM 18:3 KJV

My Father, my strength, and my Redeemer, I cannot save myself from all that terrifies me. I cannot save those who love me and look to me for protection. The world presses in on me and defeats me, despite my best efforts, until finally I call on You for help and find You there, just waiting for me to ask. Great are Your powers, O Lord; great is Your mercy; great is Your love.

"Here I Am"

Then shalt thou call, and the LORD shall answer;
thou shalt cry, and he shall say,
Here I am.

ISAIAH 58:9 KJV

Father, from my childhood You have never left me to struggle alone. All the years of my life You have been there to help me carry any burden I must bear, whether it is physical, emotional, or spiritual. I call out to You, and You answer, just as my mother always did. She knew my voice and could pick out my cry from a babble of voices; You know my heart. When I cry out to You, You are there, just behind my shoulder, ready to catch me if I fall, ready to support me if I stagger. When my strength fails, Yours is always sufficient. Thank You for Your constant love and care, for picking out my cry and never failing to rescue me.

FEAR NOT

God is our refuge and strength,
a very present help in trouble.
Therefore will not we fear,
though the earth be removed,
and though the mountains be carried
into the midst of the sea.

PSALM 46:1–2 KJV

*W*hen troubles come, I never have to face them alone. Thank You, Lord, for always being with me as my refuge and strength. Friends can fail, families can split apart, and my whole world can be shaken to its foundation— leaving me dazed and disoriented—but You never change. Your truths are forever. You do not shrug off my concerns and move on—You are "a very present help in trouble," standing firmly at my side whatever happens, guiding my actions, and giving me the strength to carry on. When all else fails, when friends and family desert me, I put my trust in You and am never disappointed.

Humble Prayer

When he maketh inquisition for blood,
he remembereth them:
he forgetteth not the cry of the humble.

Psalm 9:12 KJV

*H*ow many times, Lord, have I wondered if You heard my prayers? When wickedness surrounds me, and You don't seem to act, I blame the entire world or begin to think Your ears are closed.

If pride has caused my troubles, show me where it lies in me, Holy One. Humble my heart before You, so I can admit my guilt.

But if I must simply await Your moment for justice, let humility bring patient expectation that You will remember and act. You hear every breath of my cries when I obey You.

The LORD is far from the wicked,
but He hears the prayer of the righteous.

PROVERBS 15:29 NKJV

This verse fills me with awe, Lord, when I think that You want to listen to *my* prayers. Many call on You out of pride-filled hearts, and You cannot heed. But because I gave my life to You and want to hear Your voice, You always hear my cries.

Speaking to You in prayer gives power to my life. When I turn to You in trouble, I tap into Your strength. Though I may not get an expected answer, You often give me even more than I ask. Better responses seem to be Your specialty, Lord. So draw me close to You. When I seek the desires of Your heart, You are always listening.

His Steadfastness

Let us hold fast the profession of
our faith without wavering;
(for he is faithful that promised).

HEBREWS 10:23 KJV

How could I trust You, Lord, if I had not seen how faithful You are to Your people? The testimony of the Old and New Testaments shows the world that You have never deserted those who believed in You. Because they experienced Your faithfulness, today people still follow You through the darkest situations, relying on Your promises.

Like Your long-ago followers, I want to cling to You. Let me not waver in my faith as I follow You. May my life become a testimony to Your faithfulness.

But you are near, O LORD,
and all your commands are true.

PSALM 119:151 NLT

Thank You, Lord, for being near to me even when trouble stands on my other side. Nothing, not even all this world's pain, could be closer than You.

Thank You, Jesus, for this double promise that You always stay by me and never change Your truths. Your promises of care and protection never alter. They were true before I experienced loss, they are true today, and they will be true forever.

Your faithfulness and nearness in all my trials deserve all my praise, Lord. No one stands by me like You. There's nothing You won't do for me as long as I'm faithful, too. Help me walk with You, following Your commands all my days.

A Bright Future

He who goes forth bearing seed and weeping
[at needing his precious supply
of grain for sowing]
shall doubtless come again with rejoicing,
bringing his sheaves with him.

PSALM 126:6 AMP

When I look at my future and things seem black, You remind me, Lord, that You are still in charge of tomorrow, next week, and next year. Nothing I face now or in the years to come has not passed first through Your hand.

Thank You, that even when I'm weeping at all I've lost, You are planning a new harvest in my life. I need not doubt You will provide all I need.

Knowing and loving You bring such joy, Lord. One day, I will see Your vast blessings in my life and sing again with delight. Thank You, Jesus, for Your faithfulness and love that keep such promises.

Guidance

WRITTEN HOPE

For whatever things were written before
were written for our learning,
that we through the patience and comfort
of the Scriptures might have hope.

ROMANS 15:4 NKJV

When my heart begins to fail or doubt knocks at my door, You have not left me without counsel, Lord. No matter how the world attacks, the scriptures record Your love, hope, and guidance.

Thank You for giving me Your Word to encourage me when I feel down. Strengthen me in the face of doubt, and lead me in Your perfect way. Without Your Word in my heart, life would become dark, dreary, and incredibly painful. But Your truths heal my heart and teach me how to live in hope.

Help me learn more of You, Jesus, throughout my days. I never want to lose the hope You offer.

GROANINGS WHICH CANNOT BE UTTERED

Likewise the Spirit also
helpeth our infirmities:
for we know not what
we should pray for as we ought:
but the Spirit itself maketh intercession for us
with groanings which cannot be uttered.

ROMANS 8:26 KJV

Some days it's hard to pray, Father. I need Your guidance because I hardly know where to begin, let alone what to say or how to say it. Even when I have no special needs or requests and just want to praise You for all my blessings, I have a hard time finding the "right" words.

When that happens, I am thankful for Your Holy Spirit, who knows exactly what I want to say and intercedes on my behalf when my tongue fails me. Thank You, Father.

GUIDANCE

But be ye doers of the word,
and not hearers only. . . .
Whoso looketh into the perfect law of liberty,
and continueth therein,
he being not a forgetful hearer,
but a doer of the work,
this man shall be blessed in his deed.

JAMES 1:22, 25 KJV

Guidance is only useful when we listen to it and take action based on it. It's a foolish traveler who asks for directions and drives off in the wrong direction. Why bother to ask if you don't listen? Or why listen if you have no intention of obeying? Your Word is my guidebook, Lord, and I thank You for it, but sometimes I forget to act on what You teach me. Why read about sisterhood and then go out and slander my sister? Why study forgiveness if I intend to hang on to my grudges? Show me my errors, and teach me the proper way to take advice.

GETTING LOST

*I will instruct thee and teach thee
in the way which thou shalt go:
I will guide thee with mine eye.*

PSALM 32:8 KJV

I am easily lost, Lord. My sense of direction is terrible, and maps just confuse me. On days before important appointments, I go out and see if the roads I know take me where I want to go, which usually means I get lost two days in a row. I certainly need Your guidance on the road. Of course I need it in more important matters, too. Thank You for Your promise to guide me in all things great and small. Your eye is always on me, keeping me from error and ensuring that I can always find my way home to You, no matter how often I wander off the right road or face detours and dead ends.

Trust in the LORD with all thine heart;
and lean not unto thine own understanding.
In all thy ways acknowledge him,
and he shall direct thy paths.

PROVERBS 3:5–6 KJV

I never know what the day will bring, Lord. A perfectly ordinary day may end with glory or grief, or it may end like a perfectly ordinary day usually ends. I try to prepare myself for anything that comes my way, at least mentally, but the truth is, there are too many possibilities for me to even consider. All I can do is put my trust in You and live each day in the belief that You know how everything will work out—even if I don't. You will show me which way to turn. You will guide and protect me day after day. You have a plan, and although I don't know or understand it, I trust in You.

I am come a light into the world,
that whosoever believeth on me
should not abide in darkness.

JOHN 12:46 KJV

*L*ord, so many people stumble through life in darkness, afraid of what they might touch in the blackness, of what they might become. They have no sense of direction and no peace in their lives; only anger and fear keep them moving.

You stand outside the door, life-giving light in Your presence, if only they would turn the key and welcome You. You will wait there forever, if need be, eternally patient and loving. I pray they will hear You knocking on their hearts; may they gather up their courage and answer Your call, for You offer them light, guidance, and nothing less than salvation itself.

*For God giveth to a man that is good
in his sight wisdom, and knowledge, and joy.*

ECCLESIASTES 2:26 KJV

*W*isdom and knowledge working together give me the best chance of happiness. I want my surgeon to know every detail of my operation—all the facts of the procedure. I also want him to know if the operation is wise. Would another treatment be better suited for me? Am I emotionally, physically, and spiritually fit for an operation, or will it bring me more problems than it will solve? In other words, I want a surgeon who is both technically and ethically sound. If I find one like that, I have the best chance of experiencing the joy of healing. No one is perfect, but when I am in need of professional services of any kind, guide my choices, Lord.

*"He shows mercy from
generation to generation
to all who fear him."*

Luke 1:50 NLT

Thank You, Jesus, for this promise that I am not the only one to whom You have been merciful. Because I hold You in awe and respect—the proper fear all should have of You—Your mercy will follow me and all my family members who trust in You.

No matter how much we hurt right now, we can trust fully in You. You guide and direct us, no matter how deep the pain, and bring us into the peace only Your love can bring.

Pour out Your mercy on us, Jesus. We need it so deeply right now. May we trust in You for everything today.

Hopefulness

WHEN THINGS
GO WRONG

For thou art my hope,
O Lord GOD:
thou art my trust from my youth.

PSALM 71:5 KJV

*E*ven as a child, Lord, I knew that things go wrong. Parents divorce, love is lost, pets die, and friends betray. As an adult, I know there are many things I cannot control, no matter how hard I may try, and many of life's events break my heart. But still I hope, because through it all I have You. You can heal even the deepest loss.

Thank You for this hope, for allowing me to lean on You in the bad times. With hope, anything is possible.

A Lively Hope

Blessed be the God and Father
of our Lord Jesus Christ,
which according to his abundant mercy
hath begotten us again unto
a lively hope by the resurrection of
Jesus Christ from the dead.

1 Peter 1:3 kjv

I know that hope comes in many forms, Father. There is grudging hope, reluctant hope, tentative hope, even doubtful hope. It is, after all, in my nature to hope, even when hope has failed me before and will surely do so again.

But You, through the resurrection of Your Son, Jesus Christ, offer me a "lively" hope, a hope that never disappoints or fails. When my human hopes turn to dust, Your promise abides: "For God so loved the world, that he gave his only begotten Son, that whosoever believeth in him should not perish, but have everlasting life" (John 3:16).

HOPE IN GOD

Believe in God,
that raised him up from the dead,
and gave him glory;
that your faith and hope might be in God.

1 PETER 1:21 KJV

My faith can't be in things or even other people. They fail me, Lord, as I quickly realize when I put my hope in anything that is not eternal. You alone are worthy to bear my hope. When I first gave my life to Jesus, I understood that I can trust You, not only for my eternal life, but also for every earthly thing.

Today I put my hope in You for the situations I am in, for the hurts that afflict me, and for each second of my future. I trust in You, Father, that You will raise me up, too, just as You did Jesus.

For as in Adam all die,
even so in Christ all shall be made alive.

1 CORINTHIANS 15:22 NKJV

*H*ow pervasive death is in this world, Lord. No one escapes it, from the plants and animals around us to the people we love most. Since the moment Adam and Eve fell, suffering has been hardwired into our world.

No matter how impossible it is for us to escape death, it still does not have the last word. You sent Jesus to change the world's wiring by overthrowing death and offering life to those who put their faith in Him. The "unchangeable" pattern of death that we could not alter died in a moment of sacrifice, when Your Son gave His life for our sin.

I have no greater hope than this, Lord. I need nothing more. Help me cling to You alone, no matter what I face today.

"And God will wipe away
every tear from their eyes;
there shall be no more death,
nor sorrow, nor crying.
There shall be no more pain,
for the former things have passed away."

REVELATION 21:4 NKJV

*E*very sorrow gone! What a shock that will be, Lord. I can't even imagine what a world without pain would feel like. Such undiminished joy can hardly be thought of on earth.

But I am no longer earthbound. Your Spirit, filling me, offers hope for a new day when I won't even need to cry. Only good things—Your things—will surround me in eternity.

Thank You, Jesus, for placing this hope before me. I need it today more than ever.

Now hope does not disappoint,
because the love of God has
been poured out in our hearts
by the Holy Spirit who was given to us.

ROMANS 5:5 NKJV

I have a reason to hope, Lord, unlike so many in this world. Those who trust in a vague, happy future or have unfounded optimism lack the one thing they need—Your Spirit in their hearts.

Only Your Spirit, working in love in my life, never fails. Knowing You means that a frail human need not give in to the pressures of life's negative impacts. I need not fail when Your love strengthens my fainting heart.

Thank You for the hope that never disappoints, Jesus, for whenever I hope in You, I'm putting my heart in the right place.

DOUBTER'S REWARD

But let him ask in faith, with no doubting,
for he who doubts is like a wave of the sea
driven and tossed by the wind.
For let not that man suppose that
he will receive anything from the Lord.

JAMES 1:6–7 NKJV

*Y*ou promise that doubters get nothing from You, Lord. Those who lack trust receive no reward.

I easily doubt. My limited power in this world quickly convinces me of life's hopelessness. Tossed about by my experiences, not rooted in Your Word, I fail to rely on the One who controls both sea and wind.

When I haven't looked into Your face, I'm really only doubting my own adequacy. Both of us know I can't handle this on my own. Instead I need to turn my eyes to You, recognize Your strength, and cling to You alone. Once I've done that, I have all the hope I need.

Jesus answered. . ."Assuredly, I say. . .
there is no one who has left house
or brothers or sisters or father or mother
or wife or children or lands,
for My sake and the gospel's,
who shall not receive a hundredfold
now in this time—
houses and brothers and sisters and mothers
and children and lands, with persecutions—
and in the age to come, eternal life."

MARK 10:29–30 NKJV

I'm amazed by this promise, Lord. Nothing I give up on earth will not be returned, in some way, a hundred times over. On top of that, You offer eternal life.

Right now, I'm feeling disappointed with earthly things. I know they don't last long. They may cause pain and even disaster. So I'm glad I don't only have temporal benefits to look forward to. Thank You for giving me the hope I need: joy in eternity.

Joy

FUTURE JOY

Weeping may last through the night,
but joy comes with the morning.

PSALM 30:5 NLT

*E*ven when grief seems overwhelming, Lord, You encourage me to believe it will not last forever. My mind knows sorrow has an end, though my pain-filled heart feels it will never heal.

While I can't imagine joy, You look out for my future, preparing good things I can't perceive in the depths of my sorrow. When I cannot look ahead, You do it for me.

I can't thank You enough, Jesus, for watching over me; heading me in the right direction, even when I'm blinded by grief; and looking ahead, to create joy for me on earth and in eternity. Thank You for putting joy in my future. One morning, it *will* flood my soul.

JOY IN UNCERTAINTY

Thou hast put gladness in my heart,
more than in the time that their corn
and their wine increased.

PSALM 4:7 KJV

Thank You, Lord, for allowing me to celebrate, even when life is uncertain. When I trust in Your salvation, I don't have to depend on circumstances for joy. As I follow Your way and receive the blessings of Your righteousness, my heart fills with joy.

Though I may not know the outcome of everything in my life, I am trusting in You, and I know You care for all my needs. How my heart rejoices that I can trust in You!

JOY AFTER A DEATH

For I will turn their mourning into joy,
and will comfort them,
and make them rejoice from their sorrow.

JEREMIAH 31:13 KJV

*J*ust as You turned the mourning of Jacob's people into joy, You've turned my sorrow into happiness again, Lord. I cannot forget the loved one I lost, but I know You've given me these years of life as more than a time of extended suffering. There's still good to do in Your name.

You once saved me from my sins, and now You've delivered me from overwhelming grief, Lord. Sad living is not what You had in mind for believers. Blessings for those who love You have always been Your plan.

Thank You for every blessing in my life, including my days with the one I love. Help me share this new joy with others for the rest of my life.

Undeserved Pain

But if you bear patiently with suffering
[which results] when you do right
and that is undeserved,
it is acceptable and pleasing to God.

1 Peter 2:20 amp

Living in You not only gives me one joy after another, Lord, but suffering also comes my way as I obey You. I don't even have to do wrong to hurt. It's not something I understand, Jesus. The joys of Your kingdom and pain don't seem compatible, yet in Your own sacrifice they clearly draw together. Your love does not deny the reality of hurt.

I can't understand it all, but You promise that patiently putting up with undeserved pain still has a purpose. I please You when I untiringly bear each trial, however large or small.

Help me give You that joy today, Jesus.

You will show me the path of life;
in Your presence is fullness of joy;
at Your right hand are pleasures forevermore.

PSALM 16:11 NKJV

*B*efore I knew You, Jesus, I never thought of finding joy in God. Those who don't love You can't understand the pleasures of Your Spirit. Once Your light shone on me and I accepted Your gift of new life, You became my greatest delight.

Keep me mindful of the joy to be found in You, Lord, when the world seems dark and doubtful. As trials turn my focus away, may Your Word remind me of the fullness of joy I've had with You.

No matter how sorrowful this world seems, You store up eternal pleasures I can share with You. Keep me walking in the light of Your path, pleasuring in the earthly joys You give until we share eternal bliss.

So the ransomed of the LORD shall return,
and come to Zion with singing,
with everlasting joy on their heads.
They shall obtain joy and gladness;
sorrow and sighing shall flee away.

Isaiah 51:11 NKJV

One day, all sorrow shall end, just as You promised, Lord. Time will cease in a flood of joy as You complete salvation. Now, as grief floods back on me, I look forward to that day. I'd like to see an end to the pains I've felt on earth.

Constant, unrestrained joy in You is unfamiliar to me, Jesus. Used to the sorrows of this world, I can hardly imagine what it will be like. But I trust I'll know it in eternity. Living with and delighting in You forever will make my heart sing.

This God is our God for ever and ever:
he will be our guide even unto death.

PSALM 48:14 KJV

*M*y heart is breaking, Lord. The death of someone we love is one of the hardest things to cope with. I know the loved one is in heaven, but I selfishly want that person to still be here with me. I can gain comfort from reading Psalm 116:15. Help me to rejoice instead of feeling sorry for myself.

Fill me with the joy that comes from knowing You are my God forever and ever. You won't desert me. When death does come, You will be there to guide me to a place more wonderful than I can ever imagine.

Beloved, think it not strange concerning
the fiery trial which is to try you,
as though some strange thing
happened unto you:
but rejoice, inasmuch as ye are
partakers of Christ's sufferings;
that, when his glory shall be revealed,
ye may be glad also with exceeding joy.

1 PETER 4:12–13 KJV

*M*y suffering will never approach Yours, Lord. You had power and knowledge beyond understanding, yet You willingly gave them up for my sake, dying a human death to serve as my example and salvation. I cannot imagine everything You sacrificed for me, but I thank You from the bottom of my heart.

When Your glory is revealed at the end, I pray that I might share Your joy, as You have shared my sufferings. The suffering of this life will be as nothing compared to the joy I will feel then.

Love

SHELTER IN GOD

He will cover you with his feathers.
He will shelter you with his wings.
His faithful promises are
your armor and protection.
Do not be afraid of the terrors of the night,
nor the arrow that flies in the day.

PSALM 91:4–5 NLT

Day and night, I can trust You, Lord. Whether I go out into the world or stay at home, I am protected by Your love.

Right now I could use a lot of that protection, Jesus. The world seems a scary place because of the loss I've suffered. I never know what to expect and tend to fear the worst, whether I'm facing something new or trying to redesign my old life.

Shield me, O Lord, from my own fears. Give me the trust in You that will bring me through this trial and into deeper faith in You.

*The LORD is nigh unto them
that are of a broken heart;
and saveth such as be
of a contrite spirit.*

PSALM 34:18 KJV

Lord, my heart feels broken. Life hasn't turned out the way I expected, and I feel worn and overwhelmed.

I confess I haven't followed Your will, and my will has not turned out well. Please forgive me, Lord, and make my life new. Turn my heart from its self-centered path onto one focused on You.

Praise You, Lord, for Your love that saves me. Thank You for caring for my soul.

Conquering Love

God hath not given us the spirit of fear;
but of power, and of love,
and of a sound mind.

2 Timothy 1:7 kjv

I hear a noise at night, and my heart pounds. Children cry when the lights are out. Someone makes a threat. There are gunshots. We hear horrible things on the news. I tremble inside when I think of what could happen.

This isn't from You, Lord. This verse talks about power, love, and a sound mind. I know that those *are* from You. Because of Your power and Your love, I can have a sound mind and the peace that passes understanding.

You are our tower of strength, our stronghold. We can shout and sing and praise You for that promise.

GOD'S REDEMPTION

Israel, put your hope in the LORD,
for with the LORD is unfailing love
and with him is full redemption.

PSALM 130:7 NIV

Thank You, Jesus, for Your unfailing love that reached down and drew me in. I've learned that Your saving work didn't touch me for only a moment; it reclaimed every second of my life—even the bad ones. Whatever trials I pass through, You remain beside me, working out Your total redemption. Hope need not wait for eternity; it's evident in my daily experiences.

Help me to faithfully trust in You, Lord. In nothing else will my future, through eternity, be bright.

*"No, the Father himself loves you
because you have loved me
and have believed that I came from God."*

John 16:27 niv

You remind me, Lord, that no matter what the state of my earthly family, You remain my eternal Father. When a parent fails me, leaves this earth, or simply can't help me because of earthly limitations, I am not left adrift. You still love me, direct me, and guide my steps.

I'm so glad I'm part of Your family, Father, because You bought my life with Your Son's blood. Though my love is infinitely less perfect than Yours, my feeble response is enough for You. You pour out love on me because I've accepted Jesus in faith.

I have so little to offer, Lord. But what I have is Yours. Thank You for Your love.

COVENANT LOVE

"Therefore know that the LORD your God,
He is God, the faithful God who
keeps covenant and mercy for
a thousand generations with those who love Him
and keep His commandments."

DEUTERONOMY 7:9 NKJV

*Y*ou are so faithful, Lord. Compared to Your fidelity and mercy, the human capability to stand firm and keep promises falls far short.

I'm amazed You chose to love me and make a covenant with me, and I don't feel worthy of such a gift. Despite my failings, You desired a relationship with me. Even when I have fallen short of Your will and gone against Your Word, You've encouraged me to turn again and keep the commandments You made for my benefit.

Your faithfulness awes me, Jesus. Through Your Spirit, I want to stand as firm in all I do. Help me do that today.

LOVE'S COURAGE

O love the LORD, all ye his saints:
for the LORD preserveth the faithful,
and plentifully rewardeth the proud doer.
Be of good courage,
and he shall strengthen your heart,
all ye that hope in the LORD.

PSALM 31:23–24 KJV

*W*hen my courage seems so small and slips away, when sin seeks to pull me from Your path, Lord, remind me of these verses. I need only trust in You, the One who keeps me safe and brings good things into my life. You reward my feeble efforts and multiply them through Your strength as I simply love You and respond to You in faith.

I want to be strong—in You and for You. Give me courage each day. When evil seems to abound and sin distracts me from Your way, thank You that Your love abounds still more.

Healing Love

I will heal their backsliding,
I will love them freely:
for mine anger is turned away from him.

Hosea 14:4 KJV

Even though I've slid away from faith, thank You, Lord, that I can hang on to this promise, which says You still love me. All I need to do is turn to You again for forgiveness.

Forgive me, Father, for my double-mindedness. Part of me wants to believe You, but fear and doubt have drawn me away from Your love. I don't want doubt to destroy my love for You. Heal me from the things that would separate us.

Yours is a wonderful love that does not count wrongs. Help me live in that love every day.

Patience

Endurance

But he that shall endure unto the end,
the same shall be saved.

Matthew 24:13 kjv

Lord, I must admit that words like
patience and *endurance* aren't my favorites. They
make me think of gritting my teeth and bearing up under troubles—and I never look forward to troubles.

Give me Your vision of patience and endurance, Jesus. You came to earth and bore my
sins, when heaven was Your rightful home. You
endured much on earth so that I could relate to
You. Help me see the value in patiently endur-
ing hardship. I look forward with joy to eternity with You. Strengthen me, Lord, to be
patient until that day.

Impatience

Yea, I have spoken it,
I will also bring it to pass;
I have purposed it,
I will also do it.

Isaiah 46:11 KJV

*L*ord, forgive my impatience. I know You are faithful from generation to generation; I have no need to doubt that Your promises will be fulfilled. Yet I am like a little child on a long drive, asking, "Are we there yet?" anxious to be done with the tedious journey.

Unlike a vacation trip, my journey may go on for years. Some days I feel I will never get there, never see Your promises fulfilled. Even when one promise comes true and I reach one milestone on my path, I still worry about what's around the next bend. Some days I stamp my feet in impatience, while other days I fear the journey's end. Be patient with me, Father. This is all new territory for me.

TWO TYPES OF PATIENCE

For what glory is it, if,
when ye be buffeted for your faults,
ye shall take it patiently?
but if, when ye do well,
and suffer for it,
ye take it patiently,
this is acceptable with God.

1 PETER 2:20 KJV

*F*ather, I find it "just" when I suffer for my faults, so I bear it with patience. But You remind me that this type of patience brings no one any glory; I just got what I deserved.

Other times, though, I find myself suffering because I did the right thing, and it brought me only trouble. Now I have good reason to complain, and my patience under suffering becomes a virtue that glorifies You. Teach me the difference between these two types of patience, loving Father. Protect me when my work for You causes me pain, and help me to bear it for Your sake.

THE SECOND COMING

Be patient therefore, brethren,
unto the coming of the Lord. . . .
Stablish your hearts:
for the coming of the Lord draweth nigh.

JAMES 5:7–8 KJV

*S*ometimes, Lord, when trials surround me, I wish You would come this very minute. Even when I feel less pressure, I look forward to being at home in You. But You have another plan: You're teaching me to remain firm in the middle of struggles. It's not a lesson I enjoy, but it's one I know I need.

I want to get the benefit of patience, Lord, without the struggles. Change my heart to wait on You quietly and without complaint, so that I will be ready for Your coming.

THE PATIENCE CHALLENGE

Love is patient, love is kind.
1 CORINTHIANS 13:4 NIV

*M*y loving isn't always patient, Lord. Even trying to love myself rightly, in the face of failure, I quickly run into a block of impatience. When others challenge my ability to love, patience becomes even more difficult.

But You are always patient, kind, and caring. Your love never flags. Even when I haven't deserved it, You've offered me second chances and moments of repentance.

That kind of attitude, offered to the world, can change lives if I pass it on. I want to reflect Your love, poured out so generously on me. Though I may not feel I do it well now, I want to become patient. Help me grow in Your patient love, beginning today.

PATIENCE'S END

*Better is the end of a thing
than the beginning of it,
and the patient in spirit is better than
the proud in spirit.*

ECCLESIASTES 7:8 AMP

At the end of almost anything, I'm glad when I've shown patience instead of pride. No matter what the issue, Lord, pride lands me in trouble, while patience paves the way for good things.

On my own, I have to admit I'm not very patient. Especially when I'm under pressure, I want things now, not later, and I want people to do things my way, not their own. But when Your Spirit controls my life, I relax, accept another way, and live in Your peace. Control of everything lies in Your hands.

No matter what trials I face today, make me patient, Lord.

SLOW DOWN

*The thoughts of the [steadily] diligent
tend only to plenteousness,
but everyone who is impatient and hasty
hastens only to want.*

PROVERBS 21:5 AMP

Thank You for reminding me, Lord, that patience has its own deep benefits. When I want to hustle through this world, avoiding the stoplights, I seek the "good life" but miss out on Your best. Your halts along the way are intended to help me experience the best You designed for my life.

Trials that come with patience aren't fun. But blessing, not fun, has always been Your goal. My hurried pace seeks to avoid pain, setting its own pleasure-filled agenda for life. In doing so, it misses untold blessings You planned for me.

Don't let me miss Your best blessings. Slow me down to do Your will, Jesus.

AFFLICTION

Rejoicing in hope; patient in tribulation;
continuing instant in prayer.

ROMANS 12:12 KJV

I'm trying to be joyful in the hope I have in You, and I've been faithful in prayer, Lord. It's the having patience in affliction that is hard. When I hurt, I want the pain to stop immediately—not after I've learned the lesson I need to learn.

As I learn to rest in You, Lord, renew me. Give me the ability I need to be patient, no matter what trouble is around me. Let my joyful hope and my faithful prayers build up my patience.

Peace

PEACEFUL WAY

When a man's ways please the LORD,
he maketh even his enemies
to be at peace with him.

PROVERBS 16:7 KJV

*L*ord, You know I want my ways to please
You. Serving You is the greatest thing I can do
with my life. As an added benefit, You have
promised that because I obey, You will smooth
my path. Even my enemies will become
peaceful.

I've already seen Your promise at work
in my life. Sometimes, when life seems to be
getting rough, I pray—and the path becomes
smooth before me. Issues I thought would
become real problems turn into nothing at all,
and I know You have answered my prayer.

Thank You for Your peace, which goes
before me every day to bless my life.

*But the meek shall inherit the earth;
and shall delight themselves in
the abundance of peace.*

PSALM 37:11 KJV

*M*eekness doesn't seem the key to inheriting things in this world, Lord. When I allow others to "get ahead" of me, I usually end up losing money or power. How good it is to know that, in the end, inheriting the earth isn't a matter of pushing and shoving or making sure I get what's "due" me.

Even if I don't inherit much today, give me the abundant peace You promise—the peace of knowing that I've done Your will. Someday I know I'll have a "plot of land" in Your kingdom.

Rest in God

The LORD replied,
"My Presence will go with you,
and I will give you rest."

EXODUS 33:14 NIV

*W*hen Moses wanted to know more
of You, You gave him this promise, Lord. I've
learned the truth of it, too. When I'm close to
You, I feel a deep rest. Challenging circumstances don't disturb me much when I'm at
peace in You.

I don't have to lead a nation, as the prophet
did. I may not be great or famous, but You still
ask me to draw near and feel the calm You
give. As Your child, I am asked to draw ever
closer to You, day by day.

Today I need Your presence, Lord. Help
me rest in You always. Like Moses, I'm nothing on my own.

THE WAY OF PEACE

The fruit of that righteousness will be peace;
its effect will be quietness
and confidence forever.

ISAIAH 32:17 NIV

When I walk in Your right ways, You promise I can live in quietness and confidence, Lord. My life may not feel that way right now. Confusion seems to hold sway, instead of peace. But I still trust this is not the way my life will always continue. As I believe in You, even when I cannot see the results of faith, I grow the tree of righteousness. Soon it will flower into quietness and confidence, and my life will be blessed.

Thank You, Jesus, for Your faithfulness to me. When I can't see the path ahead, You point me in the right direction, and I am blessed in Your way of peace forever.

HEART GUARD

Be anxious for nothing,
but in everything by prayer and supplication,
with thanksgiving,
let your requests be made known to God;
and the peace of God,
which surpasses all understanding,
will guard your hearts and minds
through Christ Jesus.

PHILIPPIANS 4:6–7 NKJV

*W*hen my heart's hurting, I should pray first, Lord. How often do I remember that— or feel like praying when my mind's distracted with worry?

I can't live on painful emotions because they get me nowhere. But trust, placed in You, offers an influx of peace and hope, no matter what I'm facing.

When anxiety floods my soul, Lord, send Your Spirit to my heart. I need Your peace to guard me day by day.

FOREST FIRE

Now the Lord of peace himself
give you peace always by all means.

2 THESSALONIANS 3:16 KJV

*P*eople seem incapable of living in peace, Father. Wars flare up in one location, die down, then appear elsewhere, like a forest fire that never dies. While no worldwide fire burns and destroys today, for which I thank You, this world's disturbances never seem to end.

But while we are incapable of assuring peace, You are capable. Open my mind and heart to Your will and guidance; help me live as a citizen of a righteous nation; put out the forest fire of war. Bring lasting peace and justice to the world You love so much.

PERFECT PEACE

Thou wilt keep him in perfect peace,
whose mind is stayed on thee:
because he trusteth in thee.

ISAIAH 26:3 KJV

*P*erfect peace. "Lord, we live in a world of turmoil. There doesn't seem to be any peace from the small neighborhood to the international level. Fighting. Wars. Bombs. Threats. How can there be any tranquility found anywhere? No earthly army can protect us from harm.

Yet, this verse promises that when we trust in You we will experience peace. The peace that passes all understanding is ours for the asking. Despite wars and rumors of wars, our reliance on You can bring unexplainable contentment.

Lord, help me see peace as a core of calm deep inside. No matter what happens to upset us on the surface, You are in our innermost being, bringing peace and comfort. Thank You that we can always trust You.

TRUST IN GOD

In peace I will both lie down and sleep,
for You, Lord,
alone make me dwell in
safety and confident trust.

PSALM 4:8 AMP

*B*ecause I can rest assured You are caring for me, I sleep peacefully, Lord. I need not keep myself awake nights, worrying about my life, relationships, or future troubles. If I wake, I can turn to You in prayer and receive comfort from You. No matter what happens, You guard me and keep me from harm.

Thank You, Lord, for giving me Your rest and peace, despite the troubles I have faced. When I'm connected to You, Jesus, I have nothing to fear!

Praise

GOD'S GRASP

"And this is the will of him who sent me,
that I shall lose none of all those he has given me,
but raise them up at the last day."

JOHN 6:39 NIV

Because I'm Yours, Lord, chosen for eternity, I live in confidence that even serious loss can never steal my most important treasure. Your grasp on my soul is not so weak that anyone or anything can part us.

I may lose many temporal things. You've never promised homes or bank accounts will remain. They're only given to me to use for a while to benefit Your kingdom.

But any heart You hold, You keep forever, firm in Your hand. In eternity, I—and all who put their faith in You—will be lifted up into an infinity of praise and worship for You alone.

Thank You, Lord, for holding to me tightly in love.

SATISFIED

The poor will eat and be satisfied;
those who seek the LORD will praise him—
may your hearts live forever!

PSALM 22:26 NIV

*A*nyone, even the poorest soul who honestly seeks You, becomes filled with Your love, Lord. You never turn away a hurting heart looking to You for salvation.

Though I've experienced Your saving grace, my heart sometimes still feels empty, Jesus. But it's never Your fault. You offer many reasons to receive my praise; You fill me with Your love, life, and blessings. If my heart echoes with doubt, it's because I have not turned in trust to You.

I want to be satisfied with the blessings You've prepared for me, Lord, and share them with others, too. Daily turn my heart to Your truths, and help me speak Your praises to the world.

GREAT LOVE

For great is his love toward us,
and the faithfulness of the LORD endures forever.
Praise the LORD.

PSALM 117:2 NIV

I have a lot to praise You for, Lord, if I look clearly at my life and the blessings You've poured out on me. One sorrowful event can't close the door on all You've done for me in the past and Your continued provision for me.

Nor have You turned Your back on me in a time of grief, for as I've turned to You for comfort, You've responded generously. As I share my pain with You, Your loving Spirit fills me with comfort.

Your love has been great to me, more than I could ever deserve. I praise You for the love and faithfulness You've poured out in my life. Thank You, Jesus.

Rejoice in the Lord

I will be glad and rejoice in thee:
I will sing praise to thy name,
O thou most High.

Psalm 9:2 KJV

O thou most High"! When I put into perspective that You truly are the most high God, how can I help but rejoice in You? It is only because of You that I live and breathe. It is because of Your love that I was placed into a family who loves me deeply. And it's Your marvelous grace that took me into Your arms and made me Your child.

Father, praising You and rejoicing in You must be high on my priority list. Proclaiming Your love to others must never be lacking in my life. Thank You that I am able to rejoice in You!

I waited patiently for the LORD;
and he inclined unto me,
and heard my cry.

PSALM 40:1 KJV

What a rich promise is in this verse, Lord! If I wait patiently, You will listen and hear my cry. Psalm 40:2 talks about being in miry clay. How many times have my troubles dragged me down like clinging clay, yet You were there to rescue me!

Put a new song in my mouth, Lord. Let others see me being patient and waiting on You, no matter what difficulty I'm facing. Help them learn the same song of joy that You are giving me. Together we can sing Your praises to all those around us. You hear us, Lord. You are our mighty Savior.

When I learn to be patient and trust in You, I know that You will hear my cries and I will be blessed. Thank You for this blessing.

CALLED INTO THE LIGHT

Ye are a chosen generation,
a royal priesthood, an holy nation,
a peculiar people;
that ye should shew forth the praises
of him who hath called you out of darkness
into his marvelous light.

1 PETER 2:9 KJV

*L*ord, I can't believe it. Scripture says that You chose me from the foundation of the world. From the beginning of time You knew I would one day belong to You. It's too much for me to comprehend. You, the God of all creation, chose me to be made holy through the blood of Your Son, Jesus. You set me apart, Lord.

My praises are so inadequate to express what I feel for You, for the mighty and wondrous thing You've done for me. I probably will never understand what You saw in me.

To You, Lord, I am precious. To me, You are beyond words. I praise You, Lord, with all my being.

I will freely sacrifice unto thee:
I will praise thy name, O LORD;
for it is good.

PSALM 54:6 KJV

Lord, I can barely talk for the lump in my throat. Tears burn my eyes—not tears of grief but tears of joy and humility. I have been given such a gift today.

You know the trial I've faced. Today I heard my children pray for me. The words were so simple and heartfelt I was overcome, Father. The sacrifice You have allowed me to make in teaching them to talk to You, and follow You, has given them an understanding of who You are. They know You listen to and answer their prayers.

I want my life to be a sacrifice for You, Lord. Help me live a life of praise for You before my children. Guide me in showing them how to make the sacrifice of praise to You.

MORE REASONS TO BE THANKFUL

I thank thee, and praise thee,
O thou God of my fathers,
who hast given me wisdom and might,
and hast made known unto me
now what we desired of thee.

DANIEL 2:23 KJV

*F*ather, like Daniel, I thank You for answers to prayers. In my life, these answers are many. You've given me wisdom as You promised. You've provided financially and physically, even when the situations seemed impossible. It is wonderful to know I have a God who delights in hearing and answering my prayers. I am glad to be able to give thanks. I want my heart to continually be filled with praise and thanksgiving to You. Keep me anchored in the thought that all You do is for my good and for Your glory. Only You are deserving of my praise and adoration. Accept my heart—a heart that is full of thanksgiving!

Provision

GOD'S PROVISION

The young lions do lack,
and suffer hunger:
but they that seek the LORD
shall not want any good thing.

PSALM 34:10 KJV

Gracious Lord, thank You for Your faithfulness in providing for those who follow Your way righteously. I know every creature of this earth will face difficult times sooner or later. Even the strong may go hungry, but You are faithful to meet my needs.

When You have blessed me by Your provision, remind me to share the blessing with others less fortunate than I am, so they will have the strength to continue in the faith through my generosity. Help them see that Your provision may come in many forms, from many sources, but every good thing comes from You.

Delivered!

For he will deliver the needy who cry out,
the afflicted who have no one to help.

PSALM 72:12 NIV

*W*hen I feel helpless, I'm really not, Lord. No one who has Your aid is alone and without support.

Not only do You stand beside me when I'm in trouble or pain, You promise to deliver me. Whether I need financial, spiritual, or emotional help, You provide all I require. The only reason I could lack anything I truly need, Jesus, is that I've forgotten to ask You. Keep me in devoted connection with You, sharing every need, and I will never be needy or lost in affliction.

Thank You, Lord, for caring for all my needs and hurts. You are always faithful to me.

My Blessings

And all these blessings shall come on thee,
and overtake thee,
if thou shalt hearken unto the voice
of the LORD thy God.
Blessed shalt thou be in the city,
and blessed shalt thou be in the field.
Blessed shall be the fruit of thy body,
and the fruit of thy ground,
and the fruit of thy cattle,
the increase of thy kine,
and the flocks of thy sheep.
Blessed shall be thy basket and thy store.
Blessed shalt thou be when thou comest in,
and blessed shalt thou be when thou goest out.

DEUTERONOMY 28:2–6 KJV

*F*ather, I thank You for Your promises and provision. You touch my life in every way, never denying me that which I truly need, helping me flourish. Without You, I would surely fail, but with You, anything is possible for me.

THE FRUITFULNESS
OF THE GODLY

And he shall be like a tree
planted by the rivers of water,
that bringeth forth his fruit in his season;
his leaf also shall not wither;
and whatsoever he doeth shall prosper.

PSALM 1:3 KJV

*H*ow nice it would be to be like that fruit tree, standing next to a river that never runs dry and keeps me green and healthy while my fruit matures. Conditions aren't quite that good these days. I'm surrounded by pavement and watered by runoff water. I wilt in summer and freeze in winter, so my fruit isn't exactly grade A.

Yet You promise me that if I am true to You, You will take care of me, and I will produce good fruit. What I cannot do on my own, You will accomplish, if I trust in You.

He humbled you,
causing you to hunger
and then feeding you with manna,
which neither you nor your ancestors had known,
to teach you that man
does not live on bread alone
but on every word that comes
from the mouth of the Lord.

Deuteronomy 8:3 niv

*W*hen I need to rely on You for every bite I eat or every dollar I pay bills with, Your provision becomes very real to me, Lord. I know exactly how You care for me when I see it intimately.

But food is not the only thing You feed me with, Jesus. Your Word costs me nothing, but it offers great blessing. When I meditate on Your promises, my soul overflows with life. In this humbling time, Lord, help me to feed on You. I need to be filled with Your Word today. Nothing else can satisfy.

*"Whoever does God's will
is my brother and sister and mother."*

MARK 3:35 NIV

When I do Your will, I show I'm part of Your family, Jesus. Actions tell more than any words I utter. Just as I don't want to harm my family name by doing wrong, I desire to lift up Your name, even in trials. No one should blame You for my wrong actions; never should anyone think less of You because of me.

When I find it hard to keep up the "family name," remind me I have an older brother to lean on—One who provides for me in all things.

Thank You, Jesus, for loving me enough to make me part of Your family. I want to honor Your name and lead others to do so, too.

Every Need

And my God will meet all your needs
according to the riches of his glory in Christ Jesus.

PHILIPPIANS 4:19 NIV

This promise prompts me to ask, *What do I really need, Lord?* Is there anything I really need that You have not provided?

If I think I'm missing something, let me look again to You. I may not drive the fanciest car, but You have given me transportation—sometimes in the nick of time. You give me a place to live, food, and all the other necessities. If something seems to be lacking in my life, maybe I haven't asked You for it. Or perhaps it's not the best thing for my life, and You are redirecting me.

Even in deep loss, You look out for all my needs. As I come to You, You fill my heart, my soul, and even my pocketbook. Thank You, Jesus, for meeting every need.

FAITHFUL PROMISES

Every word of God is pure;
He is a shield to those who
put their trust in Him.

PROVERBS 30:5 NKJV

*Y*ou don't make unsubstantiated promises, Lord. I know that. Those who wrote down Your promises in scripture didn't make mistaken pledges for You; every word faithfully represents Your will and Your being. So when You say You'll be my shield because I've trusted in You, I can take You at Your word.

When trials attack, I need to stand behind You, Lord, instead of running ahead and seeking to make my own defense. I trust You, Lord, to provide all the help I need whenever I face trouble. Be near me, no matter what I experience today. Whatever You give me, it will be right.

Renewal

NEW LIFE

Therefore if any man be in Christ,
he is a new creature:
old things are passed away;
behold, all things are become new.

2 CORINTHIANS 5:17 KJV

Sometimes I feel so clean, Lord, when I've confessed sin and put it far behind me. Then I know the truth of this verse. Other times, even when I'm serving You, I feel dull and slightly used.

Thank You that Your salvation reaches beyond my feelings. It doesn't matter how I feel. When sin causes me to feel doubt or dullness, You don't toss me out of Your kingdom, but call me to new faith. I need You to renew me constantly.

Make me new again this day.

HEALING

He healeth the broken in heart,
and bindeth up their wounds.

PSALM 147:3 KJV

Thank You, Lord, for healing me. I came to You in sin, and You cleansed me. My sore heart found rest in You, and my spiritual cuts and bruises became whole under Your hand.

But this world still bruises and breaks me, Lord. When I fall into sin again, it cuts my soul. Every moment of my life, I need Your healing touch. Place Your hand on me this day.

I look forward to the day when You provide Your complete healing in eternity. I want to be entirely whole, Lord God. But until then, I trust in You to heal all my hurts. Each day I come to You for strength.

Even youths grow tired and weary,
and young men stumble and fall;
but those who hope in the LORD
will renew their strength.
They will soar on wings like eagles;
they will run and not grow weary,
they will walk and not be faint.

ISAIAH 40:30–31 NIV

No human avoids weariness, Lord. You've told me that. But somehow it always disappoints me when I lack strength to accomplish my goals or give in to weakness because I'm overwhelmed emotionally. Though my mind knows this truth, I'm slow to admit my own failings.

But You have promised renewal when I hope in You. Though my situation looks dark, You're encouraging me to trust that You have all under control. In You, I overcome.

Help me soar on Your wings, run the whole race, and not faint. Only in Your strength can I find victory.

GLAD LIFE

The humble shall see [God's salvation]
and be glad;
and you who seek God,
your hearts shall live.

PSALM 69:32 NKJV

*N*ew life in Your salvation! I felt Your touch, Jesus, and joy filled my heart. But You never meant that delight to last a moment and fade. Your joy should be an everlasting theme in my daily living.

Trials often begin to squeeze gladness from my life. Overwhelmed, I feel doubt slip in and wonder what went wrong. But trouble doesn't have to rule my days. Thank You for the promise, Lord, that if I humbly turn and draw closer to You, joy will reignite.

Jesus, draw me near today. Your new life fills my heart, even in troublesome times.

Time of Refreshing

Repent ye therefore, and be converted,
that your sins may be blotted out,
when the times of refreshing shall come from
the presence of the Lord.

Acts 3:19 KJV

Forgive me, Father. I don't want to do anything wrong; yet sometimes I sin. I'm so sorry, Lord. I feel like the apostle Paul, who said he did the things he didn't want to do. So often my sins are unintentional.

I think of those times when I bathe my children. I don't just wash off the dirt that is visible. I teach them to wash all over for the bits of unseen dirt so that they will be totally clean and refreshed.

At the same time, I teach them that when we pray for forgiveness it isn't just for the wrongs we know we've done. When we repent and You blot out our sins, our burdens are lifted, we are truly refreshed, and our spirits are renewed. Thank You for the opportunity to repent.

A New Day

Therefore if any man be in Christ,
he is a new creature:
old things are passed away;
behold, all things are become new.

2 Corinthians 5:17 kjv

Every day I get to start over, fresh and clean, because I am a new person after I confess my sins and receive Your forgiveness. Yesterday I was selfish; today I can be selfless. Yesterday I was filled with deceit; today I can be honest. I may fall backward into my old sins from time to time, but tomorrow is always a new beginning, and I do learn, if slowly. I have a lifetime of new days to spend any way I choose, and I thank You for that, because I'm bound to get it wrong now and then. When I do, You wipe the slate clean as the dawn and encourage me to try again. Thank You for Your never-ending forgiveness.

*Those who live in the shelter of
the Most High will find rest
in the shadow of the Almighty.*

PSALM 91:1 NLT

*W*hat a picture of closeness this is, Lord! How far could I be from You when I rest in Your shadow? Could I find a better place to live than in Your shelter? There I lack for nothing. You house me in many blessings because I am at Your side.

I want to live in Your place, Lord, and share the blessings of Your rest. Peace, love, and harmony fill my life as I stand by Your side. You offer me every good thing, simply for sticking close to You. May I always find my rest in You, Lord. Show me how to live in Your shelter today.

We were therefore buried with him
through baptism into death in order that,
just as Christ was raised from the dead
through the glory of the Father,
we too may live a new life.

ROMANS 6:4 NIV

*J*ust like You, Jesus, the faithful dead will be raised to new life. We've seen a reflection of that coming new life in our death to sin, through baptism. Symbolically, all our wrongs were swept away in water, and we entered into Your new life.

But faith in You is not only for eternity. Every day, I live newly, putting aside sin and sharing Your promise with those still dead in sin. I cannot rest on a one-time act to claim a place in heaven. Help me make Your new life a reality through my daily faithfulness to You. Then, when I reach heaven, I will be entirely new in You.

Resolution

DEATH'S END

He will swallow up death forever,
and the Lord GOD will wipe away tears
from all faces;
the rebuke of His people
He will take away from all the earth;
for the LORD has spoken.

ISAIAH 25:8 NKJV

One day, You promise, death will exist no longer. Swallowed up, as if it had never been, this great human fear will no longer hold sway over our lives. It's hard to imagine, Lord, since in our temporal world nothing lasts.

I look forward to a tearless day when nothing wicked is in this world, so death no longer has a purpose. When sin no longer grasps at Your people, we can share Your eternal blessings.

Thank You, Jesus, for this promise. When sorrow threatens to overcome me, I know there is still hope. Help me trust in You until that glorious day.

KEEP TRUSTING

He shall call upon me,
and I will answer him:
I will be with him in trouble;
I will deliver him, and honour him.

PSALM 91:15 KJV

All I have to do to get Your ear is call on You, Lord? If I believe, You will answer? What a wonderful promise!

In my more faithful moments, I rejoice, knowing You are at my side and will bring all this to pass. I delight in Your faithfulness. But when I face trials, it's tough to hold on to that confidence. Yet Your truth doesn't rely on how I feel. Your promises rely on Your nature, not my emotions.

Jesus, I'm thankful You are Lord and are in charge of everything. You've promised to deliver and honor me, and You will. My part is to keep trusting in You. Help me do that today.

*"For the Lamb at the center of the throne
will be their shepherd;
'he will lead them to springs of living water.
And God will wipe away
every tear from their eyes.'"*

REVELATION 7:17 NIV

One day, when all tribulations end, no tears will fall, Lord. You've promised an end of sorrow for Your faithful ones.

You've been my Shepherd on earth, caring for all my needs, and I've tasted sips of Your living water—or perhaps a cup—as I've walked faithfully with You. But one day, streams will flow abundantly throughout Your land. All will be able to drink their fill and delight fully in You.

Now, as I trust in Your promise, hope wells up. Today let me sip of Your water and live on earth trusting in Your heavenly truths.

"I have seen his ways, and will heal him;
I will also lead him,
and restore comforts to him
and to his mourners."

ISAIAH 57:18 NKJV

*Y*ou are rebuilding my life, Lord, though I've been through great sadness. Once, I could not believe life would be worth living again, but You have renewed my joy and purpose.

Thank You, Jesus, for watching over me during this grief, for directing me, even when I was so confused I didn't know where I was going. My life has been permanently changed but not destroyed. Still, You are working in me, offering me blessings I had doubted existed.

Take the rest of my days, Lord, and make them profitable to You and Your kingdom. There is so much more to life than I'd imagined— especially life in You.

Good Sorrow?

*Godly sorrow brings repentance that
leads to salvation and leaves no regret,
but worldly sorrow brings death.*

2 Corinthians 7:10 niv

Lord, You've given one purely good sorrow—the one that admits to sin and opens the door to repentance. Those who feel the weight of their sins and turn to You for relief discover the joy in life You want to share with all.

This time of loss brings me much distress, but I know I have a future hope in eternity. Many who join me in woe feel deeply but have no happy expectation to ease their burden. Their sadness remains only earthly and leads to death because they do not know You.

Though my heart aches, help me offer Your hope to those lost in sadness. Together we need to find our way in You, Jesus.

*"Come to Me,
all you who labor
and are heavy laden,
and I will give you rest."*

MATTHEW 11:28 NKJV

*B*urdened—I know the feeling, Lord. Weighed down by grief, I feel as if a heavy pack—one no human wants to lift for long—crushes my shoulders. But You, the burden lifter, are not so limited. Your Word promises You can hoist this weight from me and give me rest.

I have no one else to go to, Lord. No help on earth can ease my spirit today. I desperately need the rest You offer. The more I struggle for release, the more my burden weighs me down.

Take all my sins and doubts, Lord, and exchange them for Your peace. Fill my heart with trust in my burden bearer, and make my life whole again.

*[God] redeems your life from the pit
and crowns you with love and compassion.*

PSALM 103:4 NIV

Though I feel as if I'm at the bottom of a pit, I'm thankful I do not have to stay there, Lord. While sorrow touches my life for a time, You have not given up on me. Your redemption lies ahead, even when my life seems dark.

As I turn to You in all my pain, love and compassion appear new again. Where emotional death once reigned, Your life and joy return. Thank You, Jesus, for pulling me out of the pits of sin and sorrow. Because You gave me new life, I can move beyond the pain and into new joy. In prayer, I'm taking my first step right now.

SEASONS

To every thing there is a season,
and a time to every purpose under the heaven. . . .
A time to weep, and a time to laugh;
a time to mourn, and a time to dance.

ECCLESIASTES 3:1, 4 KJV

Grief is like a season in many ways. It goes through stages, each with its own special characteristics. Some of these characteristics are brutal, Lord; others are comforting. But like the seasons, grief eventually gives way to sorrow, to acceptance, to understanding, even to joy for the time we had with the one we lost. A wise person is always prepared for grief, because it comes to all. A wise person also knows that grief does pass with time. When my time comes to grieve, Lord, be with me. Hold me up with Your mighty arms until I can stand on my own once more. Hasten the passing of my season of grief.

Strength

Refuge and Strength

God is our refuge and strength,
a very present help in trouble.

Psalm 46:1 nkjv

When I don't know where to turn, Lord, You remind me You are always my refuge and strength. If I need a safe place to hide from the world for a time, You are there.

But I appreciate that You don't let me avoid reality for long. Instead You offer real help—strength to return, strong and vibrant, to take on every challenge. With You by my side, I will not hide from life but reenter it with the ability to overcome every trouble.

Thank You for giving me the assistance I need to go on. Your help returns me to life the way I should live it—focused on You alone. Help me rely on Your strength in every trial.

Hidden Strength

I am not courageous, Lord. Like a child, sometimes I still wonder about the monsters under the bed and turn on every light in the house as soon as the sun sets. When I look at my life's challenges, I feel so small and inadequate.

Yet You promise courage and strength when I need them. Sometimes, in Your power, I even do remarkable things that cannot be explained; I can rise to great heights when necessary. After the danger is passed, my knees may give out, and I marvel how I did such wonders. Then the light dawns: You did wonders through me. Thank You for the hidden strength You give me—Your strength.

The righteous also shall hold on his way,
and he that hath clean hands
shall be stronger and stronger.

JOB 17:9 KJV

On my own, I am rarely as strong as I need to be, Lord. Sickness weakens me; cares and worry tire my mind and make me less productive than I want to be. Old age will eventually defeat my body. Even when I am physically fit, I know there is weakness in me. But You promise that I will be able to continue in Your way as long as I have faith, and I trust Your promises. Make me stronger every day, Lord, no matter how heavy my burdens may be. Show me all the good You have done for the faithful throughout history, and give me some of Your strength when my own fails. Let my dependence on You turn weakness into strength.

He giveth power to the faint;
and to them that have no might
he increaseth strength.

ISAIAH 40:29 KJV

Sometimes the world defeats me, running right over me on its way to who knows where. Caring for my family wears me out. Struggling to survive financially is a nightmare, while saving for my old age is a pipe dream. I have no power to change any of this, and sometimes it makes me angry, Lord. Please increase my inner strength. Remind me that although I seem powerless, Your power knows no limits, and You will provide whatever strength I need to see me through my current crisis.

They that trust in the LORD
shall be as mount Zion,
which cannot be removed,
but abideth for ever.

PSALM 125:1 KJV

*M*y trust in You not only brings blessings and peace, it also changes me for the better. Once I was vulnerable to fear and worry. I tried to combat these weaknesses by taking charge of my own life and finding my way on my own. I was my own responsibility; I would take care of myself. I failed often, and in response to failing, I believed that I was not strong enough or smart enough. *There must be something wrong with me*, I thought, and there was. I had put my faith in the wrong person. On my own, I am bound to fail. Now that I have put my trust in You, I cannot fail, for You are always the victor, and this knowledge makes me strong where once I was weak.

The LORD will give strength to His people;
the LORD will bless His people with peace.

PSALM 29:11 NKJV

*Y*our peace is my strength, Lord. Without it, I am pulled in many directions, uncertain where to go or how to live. But when Your serenity fills my heart, I easily head in Your direction. I know whom I serve and where I need to go. Together we walk in the eternal way.

Thank You, Jesus, for promising me Your peace, no matter whether I face trials or the best of times. My circumstances mean nothing, for Your blessing is larger than any earthly predicament.

Today, I need Your peace. May Your Spirit pour it out on my life so I can pass Your strength on to others.

Praise be to the Lord,
to God our Savior,
who daily bears our burdens.

PSALM 68:19 NIV

*Y*ou have borne this great burden for me,
Lord, or I could never have gotten through the
grief. Thank You for standing by me, directing my steps, and healing my pain. Every day,
You've provided all I needed as I have asked
for aid.

I praise You, Jesus, for taking up all my
hurts so I could continue living. Without Your
strength, I might have collapsed under the
pain. How can I give You enough thanks and
praise for Your love and faithfulness? Though I
filled the world with them, I could never ade-
quately repay You.

Help me pass on the word of Your faithfulness to others who hurt, Lord. I know they
need a burden bearer, too.

GOD, MY PORTION

My flesh and my heart faileth:
but God is the strength of my heart,
and my portion for ever.

PSALM 73:26 KJV

*W*ithout You, how could I face troubles, Lord? Alone, I'm so weak, prone to sin, and unsure of the solutions to my problems. But my spiritual and physical "failure" doesn't have to be permanent. You give me strength to continue when troubles assail me, by filling my heart with hope. As I trust in You, strength fills my entire being.

All that I am is tied up in You, Lord. Whether I face hard times or good ones, You are forever the focus of my heart.

Trials

OBEDIENCE

*All these blessings will come on you
and accompany you if you
obey the LORD your God. . . .
You will be blessed when you come in
and blessed when you go out.*

DEUTERONOMY 28:2, 6 NIV

*H*elp me remember, Lord, that when I obey You in the middle of trials, Your blessing follows me wherever I go. Today, as I face a small but difficult task, I could make a decision with long-term impact on my life, so I want to make the right choice.

As I face temptation to make excuses or disobey Your Word, keep me strong in faith, Jesus. Your Spirit's gentle reminder tells me I'm not living just for today but for eternity. Every day of my life, even when I'm hurting, Your blessing of strong faith can cling to me.

JESUS, OUR CONFIDENCE

In him [Jesus] and through faith in him
we may approach God
with freedom and confidence.

EPHESIANS 3:12 NIV

Thank You, Jesus, for Your love and willingness to sacrifice Your life for me, enabling me to come to the Father. Without Your shed blood, I'd never experience freedom from sin and would always fear the One who created me.

As Your love brings me confidently into the presence of the Father, remind me that trusting in anything or anyone other than You lands me in a lifestyle of overconfidence in myself. If that was all I had today, pain and loneliness would flood my soul.

I need Your love and guidance for my life. During this trial, strengthen my faith and help me follow confidently in Your way.

REAL PROSPERITY

Jehoshaphat. . .said,
"Hear me, O Judah
and you inhabitants of Jerusalem:
Believe in the LORD your God,
and you shall be established;
believe His prophets,
and you shall prosper."

2 CHRONICLES 20:20 NKJV

I think of a lot of things, Lord, when I ponder prosperity. A job, bank account, or investments signify I am doing well. But just as the people of Judah could not prosper without knowing You, neither can I. Faith and blessing cannot be separated.

Thank You for all the good physical things You have given me. Even in times of trial, don't let me become ungrateful. But more than that, remind me of the spiritual blessings You've offered me day by day. Without You I could never know true peace of mind and heart or experience Your deep love.

Thank You, Jesus, for all these blessings. Help me trust in You today.

*He guards the paths of the just
and protects those who are faithful to him.*

PROVERBS 2:8 NLT

*R*ight will win out, no matter what I'm experiencing today, Jesus. I can count on Your promise to guard justice and protect me because I've been faithful to You.

It doesn't always seem like that when I'm in the middle of a trial. Because I can't see into the future to understand Your final plan, I may worry that right will not be done. Help me trust in You, even when justice seems distant. Keep me faithful to You, no matter what situation lies before me.

Thank You for keeping me from harm and bringing good even out of my troubles. I trust in You for all things, Lord.

SURE CHOICE

Seek his will in all you do,
and he will show you which path to take.

PROVERBS 3:6 NLT

*D*ecisions don't always come easily to me, Lord. I may peer into the future, wondering if an alternative will turn out right or wrong. In my own power, I'm clueless. But You haven't left me on my own, helpless in the face of choice. Instead, You promise that if I heed You, You'll guide my path in the right direction. That hasn't meant I've never made a mistake. But somehow, in the long run, as I've listened, I have ended up on the path that glorifies You.

When grief overwhelms me, I need Your clear direction. Show me surely how to make the wisest decisions in this time of trial, and lead me always in Your way.

"I am the vine, you are the branches;
he who abides in Me and I in him,
he bears much fruit,
for apart from Me you can do nothing."

JOHN 15:5 NASB

*A*bide in You! How often I forget to do that, Lord, when trials rise up in my face and confusion rules my life. It's easy to forget I'm not alone and don't have to handle things single-handedly. As I handle things on my own, I often feel left out, lonely.

I want to be tapped into You, Jesus, every moment of my life. May nothing I do be separated from Your will. Connecting to You brings me many blessings—not the least of which is the joy of Your amazing love. Let me ever be Your branch, O Lord.

"Whoever finds their life will lose it,
and whoever loses their life
for my sake will find it."

MATTHEW 10:39 NIV

When I find my life in You, Lord, nothing important can be completely lost. Even loved ones who die, if they believe in You, will meet me again in eternity. Anyone believing in You can never be truly lost again. Trials may come, testing faith, but nothing separates us from Your love and the promise of eternity. Once You've written *found* on our lives, it can never be erased.

But here on earth, Jesus, I often experience and fear loss—this side of heaven, people and things can be close to me and much valued. Remind me always that this world is temporary. Only what I hold in You lasts forever. I want my life to reflect that truth as I cling only to You.

FAITHFUL IN TRIALS

"Yahweh! The LORD,
The God of compassion and mercy.
I am slow to anger and filled with
unfailing love and faithfulness."

EXODUS 34:6 NLT

*H*ow often, Lord, I've heard others grumble about how hard life is or even blame You for wrongs in this world. Have they read this verse and trusted in Your love? Probably not.

Though I know You and experience Your love, when life becomes challenging, I'm tempted to think the world is gone awry and wickedness has won. It's not true, of course. This promise of Your nature, so large and unfailing in love, has never been destroyed, even if You don't act as weak humans expect.

Though trials come, keep me mindful of Your unchanging mercy and graciousness, poured out even in the worst situations. Help me see Your work, Jesus, in everything on earth.

Understanding

With Endurance

Indeed we count them blessed who endure.
You have heard of the perseverance of Job
and seen the end intended by the Lord—
that the Lord is very compassionate and merciful.

JAMES 5:11 NKJV

Lord, I know what it is to endure sorrow, but when I look at Job and all his losses, one right after the other, I know my loss is small compared to what some have experienced.

But that doesn't mean my pain is unimportant to You. No matter what I'm going through, if I hold fast to You, Your compassion and mercy find me out. When I suffer and put my faith in Your promises, You always come through.

Thank You, Jesus, that no matter what I may go through, You are still in control of my life, and Your compassion becomes new each day.

GOD'S SHELTERING ARMS

The LORD is a refuge for the oppressed,
a stronghold in times of trouble.

PSALM 9:9 NIV

I always need Your shelter from life's storms, Lord, but sometimes I seek shelter more often because of the challenges I face. When hurts go deep, I need a place of understanding and love.

Thank You, Jesus, for sheltering me when the world pushes in and seeks to wring all joy from my life. When I receive new life from You, I go out into the world again, strong in commitment. As Your love lives within me wherever I go, Your shelter remains with me, guarding my heart in You. You are the only protection I need.

GOD'S COMFORT

I, even I, am he that comforteth you.
ISAIAH 51:12 KJV

*L*ord, I'm so glad that when others oppress me or don't understand my pain, You're still there beside me, lifting me up. With You by my side, I don't fear anything another human can do.

But sometimes it feels hard to turn to You, Jesus. My own doubts and fears interfere. Maybe I worry that You won't understand my situation. Remind me, Lord, that nothing is beyond Your comprehension. You made the earth, our galaxy, and everything that exists— and none of it lies beyond Your understanding.

Help me ask for Your comfort when I need it, Lord. I don't want anything to come between us.

HELP IN ADVERSITY

A friend loves at all times,
and a brother is born for a time of adversity.

PROVERBS 17:17 NIV

Thank You, Lord, for giving me family to help me through the hard times. Though we may not see each other often enough, or we may have disagreements or differences of opinion on how each of us does things, when I'm in trouble, my family is there for me. It's good to have someone who understands the unspoken needs of my heart and who will help me, no matter what I face.

I appreciate this gift of family that's designed for my saddest days. May it be a blessing to me every hour of my life, in happy times as well as difficult ones. Help me stand by my family members, too, whatever they're going through in their lives.

Closest Friend

A man of too many friends comes to ruin,
but there is a friend who
sticks closer than a brother.

Proverbs 18:24 NASB

*S*ometimes having many friends seems like a good idea, Lord. When I need help, I'd like to be able to get it wherever I like. But You remind me that too much of a good thing can actually be bad. I can't have close relationships with numerous people at once. Either I get burned out, or I will not have time to share honestly.

Thank You for giving me just a few good friends and one friend who is always there, always ready to help—You. Even when my best friend on earth cannot solve my problems, I go to You and find an answer.

JESUS' COMPASSION

Jesus answered and said unto her,
Martha, Martha,
thou art careful and troubled about many things.

LUKE 10:41 KJV

*Y*ou showed so much compassion when Martha asked You to send Mary back to her work, Lord. You understood that she was worried about the many details involved in entertaining. Your words demonstrated how much You cared for her and acknowledged that You knew how much she was caught up in providing You a good meal, not something just thrown together. That dinner was the way Martha chose to show her love for You. Sometimes a kind word of understanding is all I need when I feel overwhelmed, Lord. The circumstances may not change, but I feel better about my burdens when someone simply acknowledges them. Let me give the same compassion to those who work so hard for my benefit.

He who loves purity of heart
and whose speech is gracious,
the king is his friend.

PROVERBS 22:11 NASB

A pure heart and gracious speech make the right kind of friends—those who love You, Lord. That's the kind of friend worth having, and it's the kind I want, too. But even beyond that, when my heart is pure and I speak with grace, it's because You are my friend and show me how to touch the hearts of others.

Right now, in times of trouble, I've had some who have shown me their friendship. They've given me help, listened to me, and when doubt threatened, turned my heart to You again. Their pure hearts and gracious speech have comforted my soul. Thank You for their love—and thank You most of all that You have been the friend who stood by me in the blackest times.

OPEN EARS

"He delivers the poor in their affliction,
and opens their ears in oppression."

JOB 36:15 NKJV

*W*hen I'm in trouble, Lord, I certainly hear Your voice more clearly. You open my ears because I need to hear Your truths. I'm glad You give me an extraordinary ability to listen in the middle of pain. But Your help doesn't end there. You both listen to all my needs and deliver me from oppressive affliction.

Though I hate going through any hurt, You even give my suffering value. If anguish draws me close to You, it becomes a blessing. Thank You, Jesus, for walking through this trial and then ending it. You have both delivered me and made me know You well.